THE PROJECT MANAGE' POCKETBOOK

3rd Edition

Keith Posner & Mike Applegarth

Drawings by Phil Hailstone

"Project management requires a multitude of skills – from vision and planning, to monitoring, communication, leadership and, of course, delivery.

This pocketbook pulls together best practice from these diverse areas into one simple, easy-to-read booklet. Refreshingly, it has been written from a general business perspective (rather than I.T.), and is therefore applicable to anyone managing change."
Adrian Guttridge, Vice President UK & Ireland

"A lively guide based on real events that any of us may encounter in our everyday life at work or (as I found out after reading this) at home."
Johann de Waal, Director

Published by:
Management Pocketbooks Ltd
Wild's Yard, The Dean, Alresford, Hants, SO24 9BQ, U.K.
Tel: +44 (0)1962 735573 Fax: +44 (0)1962 733637
Email: sales@pocketbook.co.uk
Website: www.pocketbook.co.uk

First published 1998. Previous edition ISBN 978 1 903776 87 2
This third edition published 2019. ISBN: 978 1 910186 07 7

E-book ISBN: 978 1 907078 79 8

British Library Cataloguing-in-Publication Data – A catalogue record for this book is available from the British Library.

Design, typesetting and graphics by **zpek ltd.** Printed in U.K.

CONTENTS

INTRODUCTION 4
About this book

WHAT IS A PROJECT? 5
Project definition, project management cycle

SCOPING THE PROJECT 13
Setting objectives, stakeholder analysis and mapping, SWOT analysis, PESTLE, fishbone diagrams, information gathering, scoping yourself and the project team

PLANNING THE PROJECT 45
Considering options, force-field analysis, 5M analysis, Gantt charts and PERT diagrams

IMPLEMENTING THE PLAN 81
Control point identification, the participative approach, pause points, communication, the change process from denial to commitment

EVALUATING THE PROJECT 105
McKinsey's 7S model, questions to ask, linking to Prince2

PROJECTING WITH PEOPLE 113
Project leader or project manager? Johari window, communicate with enthusiasm

FURTHER READING 127

ABOUT THIS BOOK

Most books about project management concentrate on the process rather than the people. We felt we needed something that looked at both, since the processes are only ever as good as the people who are responsible for delivering them.

There are two areas which are covered by this book:

1. The **task** and the project management tools to overcome problems in any project.
2. The **people** and their roles, relationships and interaction.

It includes examples from projects the authors have worked on as leaders, advisors and members. It will help you if you:

- Work in or manage a team to achieve an agreed objective for other people
- Are involved in the management of tasks where change takes place
- Wish to learn team skills and their complementary project management and leadership tools

WHAT IS A PROJECT?

DEFINITION OF PROJECT MANAGEMENT

The simplest definition of project management is:

'Managing a movement from one state to another'

This could mean designing a rocket to fly to the moon or just the process of moving people and their equipment to a different part of the office or factory. It could also be the implementation of an appraisal system or a change to an accounting monthly report. The same tools and rules apply!

Each requires great skill and diplomacy and each is fraught with difficulties. There are also degrees of movement and resistance to that movement. This book will take you through the stages of a project to provide a positive outcome.

DRIVERS OF CHANGE

Why does a project arise in the first place? Usually because one of three 'drivers of change' has brought it about. These are:

1. Competitors force you to review what you currently offer if you want to remain competitive. This may mean reducing costs which in turn may reduce overheads, or you could be looking to maximise investment. Either way, it creates changes in the quality, quantity or allocation of resources.
2. Customers may be demanding quicker response times, wider means of communication, or access to your business 24/7. Change equates to a project…or two.
3. New ideas and products are thought up to target new niche markets.

You may not have initiated the project but it has been assigned to you. **Therefore, check that your objective and outcomes are in line with the driving force behind the change.**

'TO PROJECT…'

A less simplistic approach is to refer to the dictionary, where it is no coincidence that the verb 'to project' has the following definitions:

- To propose or plan
- To throw forwards
- To transport in the imagination
- To make a prediction based on known data
- To cause (one's voice) to be heard clearly at a distance

All of the above are essential aspects of managing a project, only the scale of these activities will differ, not the activities themselves!

Hence, project management is really the co-ordination of a number of essential activities, which are being performed by other people. An orchestra needs a conductor: you will be that conductor – after all, someone has to face the music!

SPINNING PLATES

Comparing the project manager to a conductor of an orchestra is, perhaps, a false analogy. After all, in an orchestra every member is playing from the same music sheet, they already possess the skills to play the tune, and there's always the opportunity for rehearsals. Still, it gives us something to aspire to!

For those of a more 'reactive' persuasion the following would be more applicable:

Imagine you are spinning many plates on the end of poles. All you have to do is to keep all the plates spinning at once, or at least catch them when they drop!

To do this you need to share the vision of the project sponsors so that you can help them to realise their objective.

WHAT IS A PROJECT?

PROJECT MANAGEMENT CYCLE

SCOPING THE PROJECT

PLANNING THE PROJECT

ANALYSE
- SWOT Analysis
- Smart Objectives
- Outcomes Defined
- Stakeholder Analysis
- PESTLE

CONSIDER OPTIONS
- Force-field Analysis
- 5 Cs of Decision-making
- 5 M Analysis
- Gantt Charts
- PERT diagrams

REVIEW
- McKinsey's 7S
- Traffic Light
- Prince2 Elements
- Scoping Tools

PLAN OF ACTION
- Group Norms & Change Model
- Control Point Identification
- Pause Points
- Fire Prevention List

EVALUATING

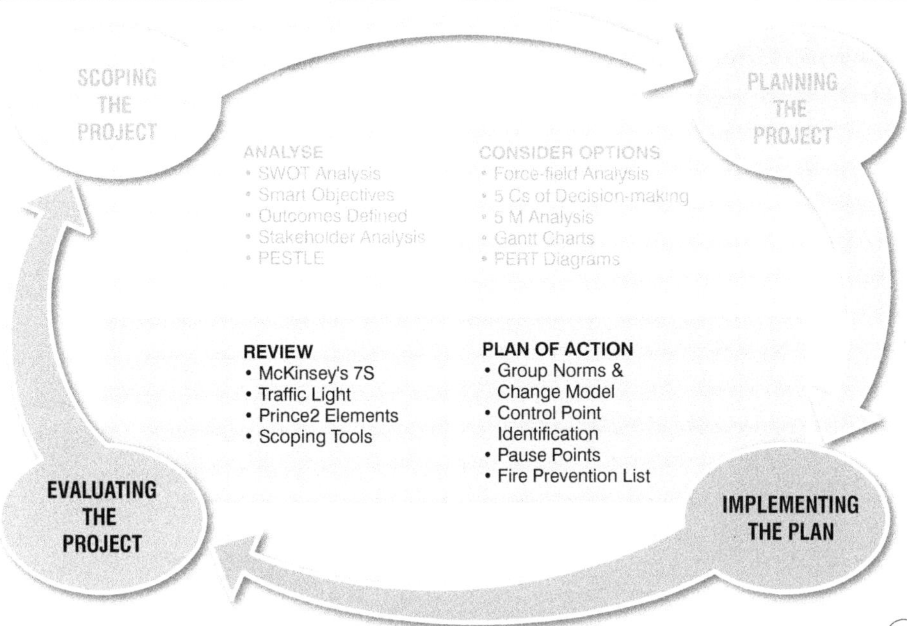

SCOPING THE PROJECT

PLANNING THE PROJECT

IMPLEMENTING THE PLAN

EVALUATING THE PROJECT

ANALYSE
- SWOT Analysis
- Smart Objectives
- Outcomes Defined
- Stakeholder Analysis
- PESTLE

CONSIDER OPTIONS
- Force-field Analysis
- 5 Cs of Decision-making
- 5 M Analysis
- Gantt Charts
- PERT Diagrams

REVIEW
- McKinsey's 7S
- Traffic Light
- Prince2 Elements
- Scoping Tools

PLAN OF ACTION
- Group Norms & Change Model
- Control Point Identification
- Pause Points
- Fire Prevention List

PROJECT MANAGEMENT CYCLE

The premise of the cycle is that there are questions to be asked **at the outset** before planning can even begin. Usually, the time devoted at this stage is wholly inadequate as the rush to have something tangible – like a plan – gathers force. Instead, proper tools should be used that provide the answers to the way forward. Otherwise, when you get to the end of the project, you can bet questions will be asked!

Planning is important to ensure that everything gets done and you are achieving your objectives or, in other words, that you are actively working towards your key results areas and not just reacting to situations as they arise.

By applying the project management cycle as shown and by writing down your findings at each stage, you can show the difference that you and the project are making, and keep the project in perspective.

This cycle provides the structure for the topics addressed in this book.

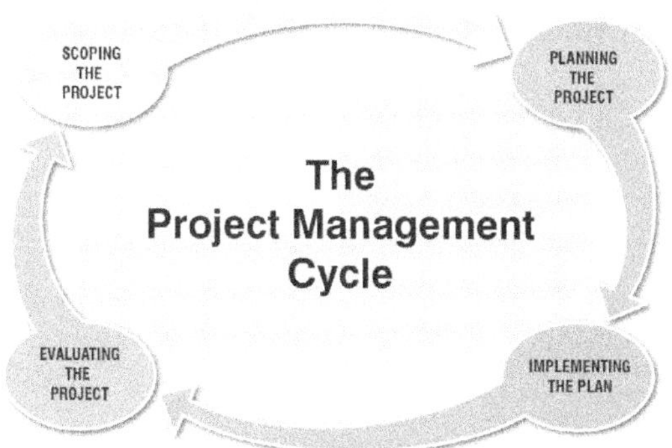

SCOPING THE PROJECT

PROJECT MANAGEMENT CYCLE: STEP 1

Scoping the project is the first step once the project has been assigned, and is the point at which we prepare the ground. It is also the point from which things could go drastically wrong if it is not carried out properly. There is a tendency with many people to call meetings immediately to pull the plans together; yet, if the overall objective and outcomes are not defined and confirmed, all the effort involved in planning may be wasted. How often has 'they moved the goalposts' been used as an excuse when, in fact, they were never fixed in the right place to begin with? This step requires:

Setting objectives: collect facts, information, opinions, needs; question assumptions; define what's in and what's excluded.

SWOT analysis:
S trengths
W eaknesses (present/internal factors)
O pportunities
T hreats (potential/external factors)

Design the strategy and identify key areas of work/skill/resource required.

SCOPING THE PROJECT

DEFINING OUTCOMES & RESOURCES

Scoping is another way of identifying what 'the long and short' of a project is – what defines its completion and what range of activities it requires.

For example, what would be the scope of a gardening project where the lawn has to be presentable in readiness for a barbecue?

Firstly, we need to ask what it will look like when it's done well. Having defined the desired outcome, we then consider the resources required to achieve it. If the outcome were a lawn that wasn't scalped and where loose change would be clearly visible from three metres away, this could be achieved by using:

- scissors
- a scythe
- a strimmer
- a ride-on mower
- two rotary mowers working together, or
- a push mower

The factors we must also consider though are those of time, cost, quality and quantity. If time is no object and you have no money, then a pair of scissors could eventually do the job!

SETTING OBJECTIVES

Think about outcomes – what will the project look like when it's done well?
Decide what you want to achieve within a certain time period.
Think how the outcomes can be measured using the **SMART** test:

Specific	Is the activity to which the objective relates clearly defined?
Measurable	Will the outcomes sought be visible when the project task is completed?
Achievable	Is the entire task, though challenging, physically possible?
Rewarding	How will the project benefit the organisation, team or individual?
Time-bound	What is the deadline for completion?

Remember, if you haven't described the outcomes you will measure against, then you haven't done your job properly!

SCOPING THE PROJECT

SETTING OBJECTIVES

EXAMPLE

Here's an example of a **SMART** application:

To redecorate the entire downstairs of your house so that:

- The walls, ceilings, doors and window-frames are cleanly finished in your chosen colours
- There are no paint stains on furniture, fixtures or fittings
- The carpet is not damaged
- The materials and labour costs are within budget
- No cracks or blemishes are visible
- The project is completed by 5.00 pm on Friday 13 November

Would it therefore be appropriate for you to criticise the decorators if they hadn't repainted the radiators and removed them to clean and paint the walls behind? Be professional with the professionals and confirm all assumptions from the outset so you all know what good looks like!

STAKEHOLDER ANALYSIS

Stakeholders are those people or organisations who may be affected in some way by the project you are undertaking. What is at stake for them?

Use the format below to identify all the stakeholders for your project, analyse their needs, and make them measurable (third column). The more specific you can be about what your project offers, the better you will see who should be on your side … or who to win over. Some examples may be:

Stakeholder	Needs	Performance Indicators
Board member	Strategic growth/profit	Business plan/+10%
Operations director	Efficiencies/sales	£x costs/£y sales
Employees	Security/health & safety	Paid job/no injuries
Suppliers	Continuity/sales	Contract length/£revenue
Clients	Value for money/response time	Fit for purpose/KPIs/hours or days
Governing bodies	Compliance/audit trail	Audit measure/documentation

STAKEHOLDER MAPPING

You will need to consider people beyond the immediate target of the project. For example, it's easy to think of the local council and residents of an estate where you intend to site a phonemast, but what about the environmental lobbyists and cable telecomms providers? What might their level of interest be in the outcomes and activities of your project and what might increase or reduce it? Some people may have no interest until it 'enters their back-yard', then they become campaigners, both taking more interest and seeking to exert influence.

So levels of **influence** as well as levels of **interest** change during the course of a project. Individuals combine with others to form 'bodies', and they in turn join forces with other bodies or organisations to lobby key influencers and decision-makers. Campaigns can strengthen the influence brought to bear. The diagram on the next page (adapted from Aubrey Mendelow) illustrates the relationship between interest and influence. Your stakeholder mapping should identify all prospective parties within each of the quadrants so you can prepare to address their concerns.

STAKEHOLDER MAPPING

Level of Influence ↑	Low interest	High interest
High	**Potential Change Agents** Identify how your project may impact on them	**Key Players** Keep them satisfied
Low	**Indifferent** Minimal effort needed	**Back-Yarders** Keep them informed

Interest Level → (Low to High)

THE 4 STAGES OF A PROJECT

1.
Set quality and quantity objectives

Ideas, problems and issues to resolve

2.
Plan and schedule time and cost

Feasibility of objective, specify outcome and plan everything you can

3.
Implement plan

Action; delivery of the outcome specified

4.
Evaluate results of the project

Take 'delivery' of project, correct any defects and learn lessons for next time (eg: What went well, what didn't go well and what would you change?)

THE OUTCOMES APPROACH

An 'outcome' provides an objective measure that should not be open to misinterpretation. It removes subjective assessment and indicates clearly **all** the significant factors that determine success.

Quite simply, the project manager describes to the team members the **full** end result they will be assessed against before they get there. Contingency and 'what if' factors should be considered at the outset. For example:

- A sales manager is required to bring in £1 million of revenue; what if it costs him £500,000 in the process?
- A programmer is tasked with setting up a particular computer program by a set date; what if another program crashes as a result?
- A driver changes the car wheel and arrives safely at her destination; what if she had left the damaged wheel at the roadside or had damaged the car in the process?

Consider all the things you consciously look for but never openly express. **There should be no surprises for the team about what you are measuring!**

SWOT ANALYSIS

Use **SWOT** to identify the conflicts and forces at work, both internal and external for a specified ability.

You will need to establish how things are now (the current situation) and also where you want them to be by the end of the project.

It is often said by experienced project managers that whilst internal strengths and weaknesses do not tend to change rapidly, external opportunities come and go **but** threats usually remain.

SWOT ANALYSIS

Strengths/Weaknesses

These are always your own or your organisation's (internal) strengths and weaknesses. The following is a list of key aspects to consider:

- People/management expertise
- Facilities/building and equipment
- Technology
- Marketing/sales development skills
- Reputation/image
- Financial resources

Opportunities/Threats

External factors can cause your project to fail if you don't consider all the 'what ifs'. The following factors will affect how you approach the project, allowing you to be better informed at the planning stage:

- Political/social/economic changes
- Competition, locally or even nationally
- Market size and trends
- Profitability of market
- Needs that your products fulfil
- Likelihood of these needs changing

PESTLE ANALYSIS

PESTLE analysis should be used in conjunction with a SWOT analysis when examining the potential for Opportunities and/or Threats. It is a mnemonic to draw attention to those factors external to you, or the organisation, that may be perceived as positive or negative. Originally referred to as the PEST analysis, it has been brought up-to-date to reflect the explicit inclusion of more modern-day influences.

Political – the political influences on a company or project, eg: impact of changes in government, political lobbying, or even in-company politics.

Economic – those economic and financial influences on a company or project, eg: profit, margins, exchange rates, euro issues, inflation, recession, unemployment, local, regional or national economy.

PESTLE ANALYSIS

Social – those social influences on a company or project, eg: demography of markets or skills availability, local community, sponsorship, working hours, school projects and charities.

Technological – those influences new technologies have on a company or project, eg: systems, equipment, research & development, innovation, communication with markets and suppliers, accessibility.

Legislative – the impact of new laws and regulations on a company or project, eg: local authority regulations, national laws, EU and World Trade directives.

Environmental – the influences on a company or project that affect the environment, eg: disposal of waste, use of natural resources, pollution, environmental lobbying, eco-friendly policy, ISO 14000.

FISHBONE DIAGRAMS

CAUSE & EFFECT

Why not try out a Fishbone diagram to link together all the issues that have a bearing on the problem? Define the problem in the head box at the right hand side and add a bone to the left for each of the contributing factors. These could, for example, be the 5Ms (see page 53), 7Ss (see page 107) or later parts of the process.

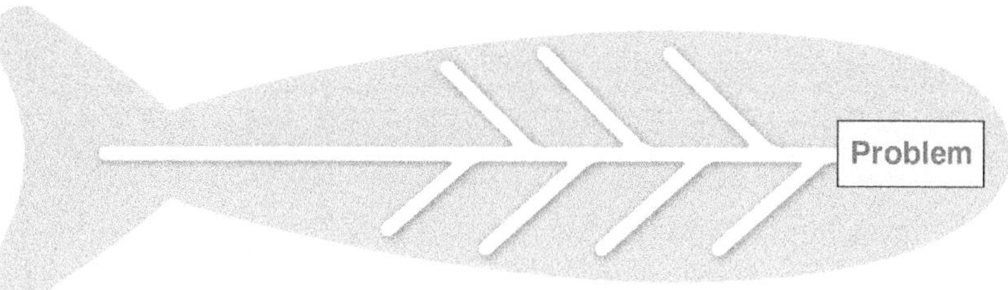

FISHBONE DIAGRAMS

SOLUTION IMPACT

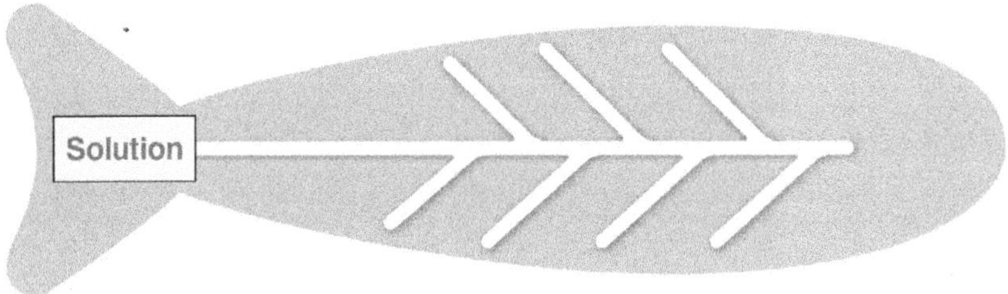

Alternatively, place the focus in the tail end to explore the effect of a solution or idea on areas labelled on the skeleton. Each larger bone could have smaller splinters attached as sub-headings of the broader label. Here, it's the knock-on effect we are looking at.

SCOPING THE PROJECT

SCOPING MEASURES

EXAMPLE

Imagine a project where you and three colleagues have to travel from London to deliver a sales presentation in Brussels. How will you go about it, bearing in mind constraints of time, cost, quality and quantity?

Travel

- Clearly, you can go to Brussels from London by many means.
- If time is no object, then walk or go by bike.
- If money is not constrained, go by Eurostar train, first class, or by plane.
- If you need to work during travel time, then take the train or ferry.
- Can you get there and back in a day?
- How much luggage do you have to carry?

Accommodation

- How close to the meeting place do you have to be (10 mins or 1 hr)?
- Do the four of you have to be together?
- Will you only need bed & breakfast?
- Is accommodation required before or after the presentation?

SCOPING MEASURES

EXAMPLE (Cont'd)

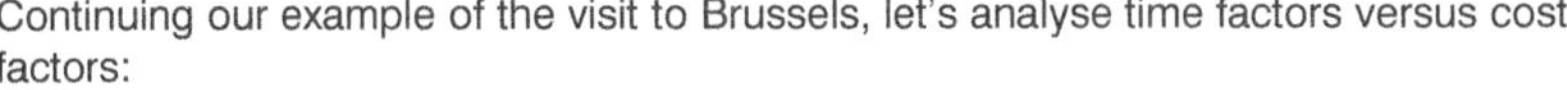

Continuing our example of the visit to Brussels, let's analyse time factors versus cost factors:

TIME	LOW COST	HIGH COST
HIGH	Walk/bike Car/ferry *B&B (1 hr away)*	Car/ferry with overnight stop *5 star hotel (1 hr away)*
LOW	Train (2nd class) *B&B (5 mins away)*	Train (1st class) / plane *5 star hotel (5 mins away)*

TIME (LOW → HIGH)

COST (LOW → HIGH)

SPONSORS & END-USERS

As much information as possible should be gathered about the wants and concerns of the sponsors and end-users. A helpful way to remember how to identify the channels of influence that may exist on a project is to apply the **DRUGS** test:

D ecider	Authorises and initiates project and agrees the terms of reference.
R ecommender	Wants change and needs to be convinced it is an integral part of the business. Projects always have friends and enemies. Ensure this person is on your side!
U ser	Implements, and influences Recommender.
G atekeeper	Experts who are listened to by Decider and secretaries/personal assistants who can limit or extend access to Decider/Recommender.
S takeholders	Can be outside the project entirely (eg: legal, moral and ethical third parties).

In a small project, the Recommender and the User could be the same person, such as an area retail manager who is changing the monthly reporting of sales from the five shops in her area.

ESSENTIALS OF COMMUNICATION

Gathering information from sponsors, end-users and other involved parties is all about communication. So when you're planning a discussion, **POURS** before you decide:

P lan	What to tell and ask
O utline your understanding	Clarify objectives and seek constant feedback
U se open questions	5Ws 1H (as illustrated)
R eflect	Use closed questions for confirmation (you have two ears and one mouth and should use them in that proportion)
S ummarise	Agree actions

THE NATURE OF ANY PROJECT

As a basis for information gathering, think **SQID** when approaching any project. See, for example, how it applies to acquiring a new computer system:

S peed of response to customer enquiries and requirements
How quickly do we need the computer system? How will it speed up our service?

Q uality of product and advice
Why do we want the new system? What must it be able to do? What must it be compatible with?

I nformation must be able to be fed in and should cross traditional functional boundaries without difficulties
Will we be able to use the new system the moment it arrives? What are the consequences of mistakes being made during the changeover? How are the desired outcomes expressed to the contractor?

D elivery time to the customer or to the next link in the supply chain must be the shortest necessary to complete the job
Is there a learning curve to experience and, if so, for how long? If we use a contractor to set us up, when could the job be done and what support will we get?

INFORMATION GATHERING

When scoping the project, the nature of the information required falls into four categories:

1. Time How much time? How urgent is urgent? What will happen if the status quo is maintained?

2. Cost How much money do you need? How much will be saved by changing the procedure?

3. Quality To what standard must the outcome be measured?

4. Quantity How many? What will happen if quality is sacrificed for quantity?

All four categories must be balanced against each other. As with all projects, sacrifices must be made to achieve the objective. The secret is to ensure that the project sponsors have weighed up the options that the project team has put to them.

INFORMATION GATHERING

1. TIME

Having defined your desired outcome, consider the questions you may need to ask in order to obtain the relevant information about the impact of time within the project:

- Q How much time is available?
- Q How much time does each key activity need?
- Q How urgent is urgent?
- Q What will happen if the status quo is maintained?
- Q What difference will the change make to the speed of information delivery or response time to a customer?
- Q Within what degree of accuracy should completion of the project take place? Are we talking days, hours or minutes?
- Q Does any stage or activity of the project have a particular deadline or restriction on time?
- Q Do different time zones have to be co-ordinated?
- Q How much notice do contractors or suppliers need?
- Q What activities can take place in parallel rather than in series?

INFORMATION GATHERING

COST

You may need to ask the following:

- **Q** What is the budget?
- **Q** Are there penalty clauses that could be imposed? (Construction projects eg: motorways were notorious for completing late and over-budget unless penalty clauses were included in the original project specification.)
- **Q** Is there funding up front or is it 'pay as you go' or cash on delivery of the system or product change? (How is cashflow affected?)
- **Q** What will it cost?
- **Q** What will it save over the longer term?
- **Q** Are 'guesstimates' acceptable for some decisions?
- **Q** Is this a 'fixed-cost' or a 'cost-plus' project?
- **Q** What detail of record-keeping is required to reclaim costs?
- **Q** Is there discount for bulk?

INFORMATION GATHERING

QUALITY

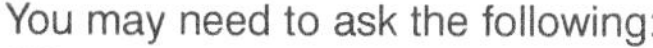

You may need to ask the following:

- What are the expressed outcomes to be measured?
- Who is measuring and do they know what they are measuring?
- Who is responsible for quality?
- When do you check for quality: at the input stage, on-going or when the project is finished?
- Are you expecting 'zero defects'? What tolerance levels are acceptable?
- What is the procedure when quality is below acceptable levels?
- What steps or procedures could be put in place to ensure quality at every stage?
- Is functionality more important than cosmetics?

INFORMATION GATHERING

QUANTITY

The following quantity-related questions may be relevant:

- **Q** How much can be produced without sacrificing quality for quantity?
- **Q** At what level of output do 'economies of scale' come into effect?
- **Q** How many people do you need?
- **Q** How long do you need them for?
- **Q** How much scope is there for 'wastage' or 'trial and error'?
- **Q** Does everyone need their own desk, computer, phone, etc?
- **Q** What's the likelihood of spares being needed?
- **Q** How much of x can we hold in stock?
- **Q** What is the turnover of staff or materials?
- **Q** Can we cope with the demand, usage, etc?

TERMS OF REFERENCE

The terms of reference for a project are an outcome of scoping, and should be agreed before the planning stage gets underway. They should be documented and should constitute a contract between the sponsor/end-user and the project team.

They can be formalised in a scoping document, the template for which should always contain the eight headings shown.

Scoping Document

1. Objectives and outcomes
2. Project stakeholders or sponsor (see DRUGS)
3. Constraints
4. Scope – what's in and what's left out (assumptions)
5. Budget/resources
6. Time-scales/milestones
7. Risks and mitigation
8. Who is doing what for whom? (Roles and responsibilities must be defined with a job specification so no one overlaps or encroaches on another's territory.)

In short, it should help to describe what the project looks like when it's done well.

SCOPING YOURSELF & THE PROJECT TEAM

In a project you will need to manage the people as well as the task. Achieving the balance will require tact and diplomacy, and not a little good fortune!

- **A people-orientated approach** requires available time to allow for everyone to participate, and for team members to navigate the learning curve which often dictates the pace of the project. This approach can inspire commitment to change and team loyalty.
- **A task-orientated approach** puts the needs of the project before those of the people, and is generally adopted where deadlines are tight. Unfortunately, as sponsors invariably want things yesterday, more and more unrealistic or compromising deadlines are set, so this becomes the norm. Loyalty and commitment are difficult to attain and crisis management may be called for.

You may not get to choose but, if you do, try to put people first. And if you can, choose the right people, as the next page indicates.

SCOPING THE PROJECT TEAM

Research by Professor Belbin shows that each individual of every team is different and, therefore, people with the same skills working on a project may behave differently. Their behaviours will affect you whether you are the project's sponsor, leader or team member.

Below, we use Belbin team styles to define the roles that people have natural tendencies to play in project teams, notwithstanding the functional skills and knowledge they bring:

Co-ordinator	Clarifies goals and promotes participative decision-making but could delegate the 'walking of the talk'
Shaper	Challenging, will drive through change but will expect everyone to change behaviour immediately
Implementer	Will turn ideas into practical actions (or scoping into plans) but may be inflexible about outcomes created by others

SCOPING THE PROJECT TEAM

Plant	Will be creative and unorthodox in approach but may ignore how the plan should be implemented
Resource investigator	Will find out how other teams make it work but will tend to lose enthusiasm once planning stage is over
Team worker	Will diplomatically encourage and support others but may avoid conflict at the expense of the project
Monitor evaluator	Will see all the options and watch for milestones but may lack the drive to inspire others
Completer finisher	Will want the change delivered on time but will want to do it all him/herself and will worry about the outcomes unduly

SCOPING YOURSELF

Before embarking on the project, it is helpful to recognise what it is that you and others on the team bring to the project. This could identify any gaps that need filling and reinforce the team spirit and self-belief. Useful questions to ask are:

- Q What skills do you have?
- Q What relevant knowledge do you possess?
- Q What did you learn last time? Write it down!
- Q Is this a secondment or are you just doing two jobs that are both full-time?
- Q What do you want to get out of the project?
- Q Who will carry out your appraisal?
- Q How will your line boss know if you have a problem or know about your success?
- Q Who cares for the needs of fellow project team members?
- Q In what situations do you work best?

"Change is something the top asks the middle to do to the bottom,"

Rosabeth Moss Kanter

DETERMINING THE RIGHT AGENDA

To help confirm the scope of the project, you should know the answers to these questions before you begin the planning:

- Q Who does your solution need to perform for?
- Q What results and benefits should the solution produce?
- Q What costs or penalties do you want to avoid?
- Q What limitations and restrictions apply?
- Q What do you want to happen?
- Q What don't you want to happen?

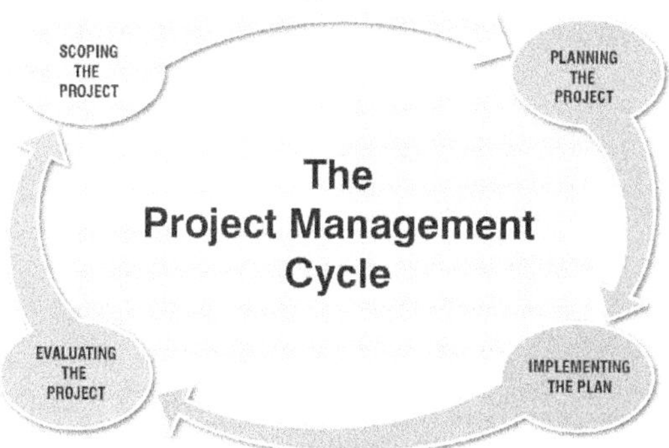

PLANNING THE PROJECT

PROJECT MANAGEMENT CYCLE: STEP 2

As we have shown in the previous chapter, there is a lot of essential information to collect and assimilate before you can even contemplate putting together a plan. If you don't know where you are heading, how can you possibly know how to get there!

Planning will involve:

- **Considering options**
  - highlighting key issues
  - generating ideas and opinions
  - using the 5 Cs of decision-making (see page 49)
  - assessing your 5 M resources (see page 53)

- **Recording the plan**
  - applying charts and graphs

FORCE-FIELD ANALYSIS

This tool works where there is a 'thorny' topic or a politically sensitive issue to resolve, such as changes to work patterns or financial packages, or wholesale changes to reporting structures which may involve management and staff needing to negotiate changes. You will need to resolve the weight of the forces favouring and resisting the change.

The key is to ensure that the size of the arrows is commensurate with the weight you give to that issue. Some arrows cancel themselves out and, therefore, leave you with a balance of probabilities as to whether you will be able to implement the change envisaged. At least you will be going in with your eyes open!

FORCE-FIELD ANALYSIS CHART

Applying this chart gives you a mechanism for highlighting key issues and identifying action plans. Our example concerns upgrading a computer system. The **driving forces** (for) are all influenced externally. The restraining forces (against) will all be internal, so you can do something about them, but what? Imagine a third column showing actions to make more of the drivers, and to overcome the restraining forces. The longer the arrow, the greater the influence it exerts. In which direction is the force stronger?

Forces For	Forces Against
Recognition of need to change →	← Loss of security
Pressures from customers/suppliers (internal and external) for quicker responses →	← Fear of unknown
	← Tradition/custom
Loss of market share →	← Fear of getting it wrong
Backlogs of work →	← Agreed working practices
Need to reduce costs →	← Established relationship with current systems supplier
Competition →	← Loss of productivity during learning curve
Incompatibility of systems across divisions →	← Reluctance to let go
Data protection requirements →	← Diversion of funds
(consider PESTLE again)	← Lack of skills

CONSIDERING OPTIONS

The 5 Cs of decision-making is a useful reminder of the process ahead of implementation:

Consider
- clarify the nature of the project, time and other constraints
- ask yourself and others what information you need
- **identify objectives**

Consult
- gather the maximum amount of information available
- call a meeting of those involved or their representatives
- **brainstorm** if necessary
- decide at which point the consultation will stop

Crunch
- review all the options and **make your decision**
- write down your implementation plan

Communicate
- provide briefings on what will happen, why, and who the decision affects
- back-up briefing with written confirmation of the decision
- make sure everyone understands when the decision will be implemented

Check
- check that the briefing is carried out
- run spot checks to monitor effectiveness
- review the impact of the decision and **take any corrective action**

RECORDING THE PLAN

Plans should be drawn up for the following:

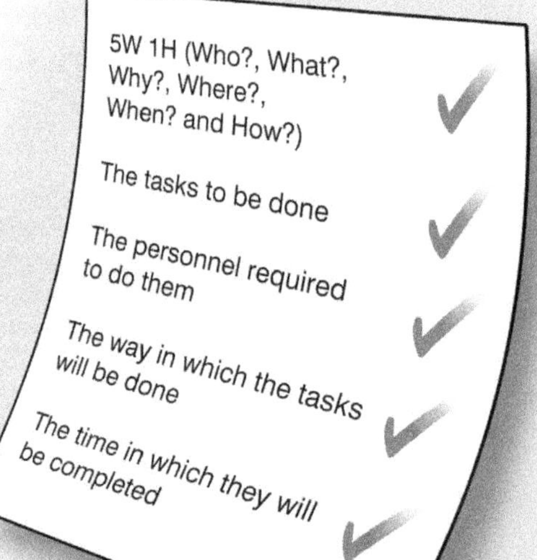

TEAM FRAMEWORK

Whether or not you were able to choose your team, as discussed under 'Scoping', getting their contributions to the planning of the project is another good opportunity for team-building. After all, plans should not be drawn up in isolation. The following are key questions that need to be asked of, and answered by, new teams:

- What makes a good team?
  - key skills (Belbin team roles)
  - effective procedures
  - stages of development and application of SWOT
- How can our team work smarter?
  - for each other
  - for their stakeholders
- How can the team identify milestones to measure and review their success en route?
- How can the team communicate more effectively...
  - with the leader?
  - among themselves?
  - with their stakeholders?
- How can the team use their human resources more effectively?
- How can the team be effectively managed?
- How will the team appraise themselves/be appraised?

PROJECT TEAM ISSUES

When you assemble your team at the outset of a project, be sure to address with them:

- Why they are here - mission
- What they will be doing - goals
- How they will recognise progress - planning the milestones, communication and feedback
- What's in it for them - recognition
- What happens when they need help - support

Ensure you get the right mix of traits, not just skills (see pages 41-42).

5 M ANALYSIS

We stated earlier that planning involves considering all the options. Some options, though, may be missed unless the project is broken down into manageable chunks, just as we did when scoping the project. One way to facilitate planning is to look at options within the 5 Ms:

- Machinery
- Manpower
- Materials
- Methods
- Money

5 M ANALYSIS

Difficulty (Problem/Obstacle)	Machinery	Manpower	Materials	Methods	Money
1					
2					
3					
4					
5					

5 M ANALYSIS

MACHINERY

- Q What PCs or tools are required?
- Q What vehicles, rooms, chairs, tables, wipe boards, etc, are required to fulfil the project?

MANPOWER

- Q What people resources will be required?
- Q For how long?
- Q How will their appraisal be conducted?
- Q How will they be managed?
- Q What skills do they have/lack?
- Q What training programme needs to be undertaken to develop the users and project members?
- Q Should they read this pocketbook before starting the project?

5 M ANALYSIS

MATERIALS

- **Q** What raw materials are required?
- **Q** Where can we get these materials?
- **Q** Is it worth spending more to get materials that are more durable, easier to maintain, more portable, etc?
- **Q** Will the new materials require changes to systems, special skills, etc?
- **Q** Will the materials be available at the appropriate time and in the right quantity?

METHODS

- **Q** What methods will be used as the 'language' around which all project discussions take place (eg: Gantt charts)?
- **Q** How will information be reported back to the project team and end-users?
- **Q** What will be the reporting lines to the project manager – daily, weekly, monthly?
- **Q** How much information needs to be reported?
- **Q** What marketing methods are required? (It may be necessary to draw up a marketing plan to sell the concept of the project, either internally or externally.)

5 M ANALYSIS

MONEY

- **Q** What financial resources are required to fulfil the objective?
- **Q** What budget has been allocated?
- **Q** What cost savings have been projected?
- **Q** What will be the short-term cost to 'prime the pump'; to get the project off the ground?
- **Q** What will be the impact of the project on cashflow?

5 M ANALYSIS

EXAMPLE

In this example the team project is to move a company of 60 people to the other side of the city. By applying the 5 M analysis, the following considerations are highlighted:

MACHINERY

- What size of removal vehicles is required? How many of each?
- Is there a need for specialist equipment to remove fixed items or to transport heavy items indoors?

MANPOWER

- Are internal or external resources to be used?
- Will a removal company be engaged to remove all of the equipment and furniture? Or will a combination of internal and external resources be better?
- Will it be necessary to get assistance from telephone suppliers with phone/wi-fi/PC cabling?
- What further help will be required?

5 M ANALYSIS

EXAMPLE (Cont'd)

MATERIALS

- Do we have the crates, cartons, etc, to pack the items for removal?
- What items actually have to be removed?
- What new materials will we require (eg: cabling and power sockets, new carpeting)?

METHODS

- Could greater use of a cheaper resource save the need for a more costly one?
- Does it make more sense for parts of the company to move first, or for everyone to move at the same time?

MONEY

- How much money is available to move the people and their equipment?
- Will the people who are moving actually conduct the move, ie: will they need to hire vans and will they be able to move the PCs and other items?
- What happens if there are breakages or C drives are damaged in the move?
- What about 'damage-to-goods-in-transit' insurance?

THE HOCKEY STICK EFFECT

You will always need more resources up to and just after the change you introduce. This is when you need to hold your nerve, as people and resources will be at their tightest and you will be under intense pressure to release people. Don't plan any holiday at this time; plan some before the major change – and three months after to recover!

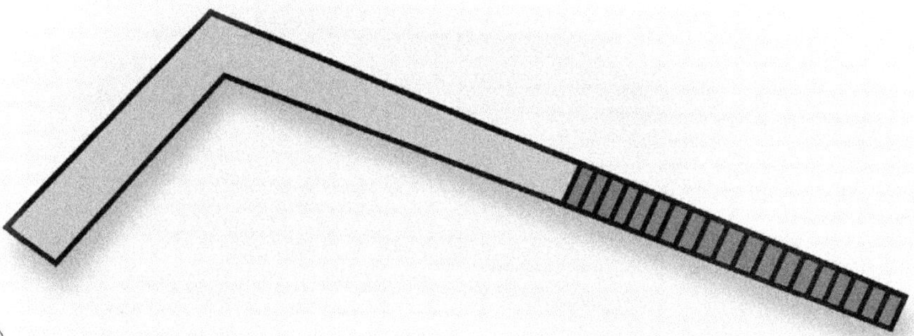

THE HOCKEY STICK EFFECT

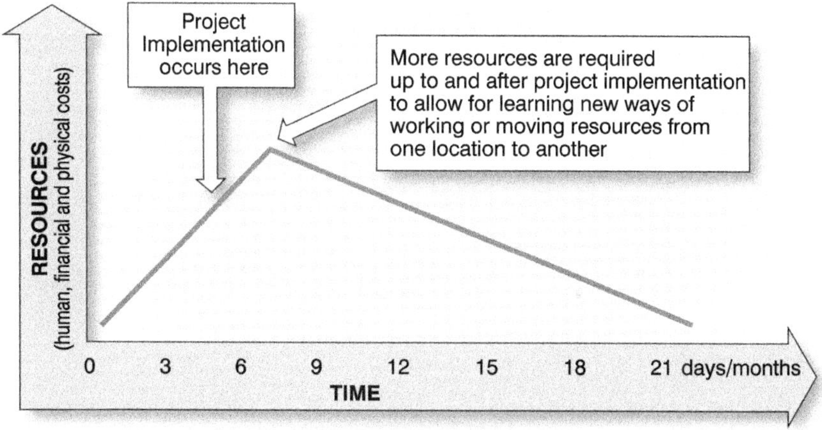

Project Implementation occurs here

More resources are required up to and after project implementation to allow for learning new ways of working or moving resources from one location to another

RESOURCES (human, financial and physical costs)

0 3 6 9 12 15 18 21 days/months

TIME

TASK OR PROJECT?

When is an undertaking an everyday management task and when is it a project? Perhaps the answer lies in the distinction we make when thinking about such issues.

When we have a defined plan, procedure or organisational system, and clear channels of communication, all of which have been in place for some time, we are **unconsciously skilled**.

However, when a project manager/leader performs tasks that are unfamiliar, undefined or uncertain, and the lines of communication are unknown, he or she will need to be **consciously skilled**.

The role of planning in project management is to make things certain, defined and clear when communicating – and create ***order out of chaos!***

The following page gives a clearer view of the key differences between task and project.

TASK OR PROJECT?

The differences between everyday management tasks and project management are:

Issue	Everyday Task	Project
Undertaking:	Familiar	Unfamiliar
Staff:	Known	Temporary
Team roles:	Established	Uncertain
Relationships:	Co-operation	Negotiable
Authority:	Clear position	Little/indirect
Information source:	Routine	New/uncertain
Attitude to change:	Desirable	Essential
Momentum:	Maintained by system	Threatened by system
Time-scales:	Extended/long-term	Ring-fenced/finite
Co-ordination:	Hierarchical	Network/matrix

GANTT CHARTS

Of all the project management tools this is probably the simplest to understand, the easiest to use and the most comprehensive. It allows you to predict the outcomes of time, cost, quality and quantity and then come back to the beginning.

It helps you to think about people, resources, dates, overlaps and key elements of the project, and you can concertina 10 separate Gantt charts into one overall chart.

A Gantt chart is a horizontal bar chart that graphically displays the time relationship of the steps in a project. It is named after Henry Gantt, the industrial engineer who introduced the procedure in the early 1900s. Each step of a project is represented by a line placed on a chart in the time period when it is to be undertaken. When completed, the Gantt chart shows the flow of activities in sequence as well as those that can be underway at the same time.

To create a Gantt chart, list the steps required to complete a project and estimate the time required for each step. Then list the steps down the left side of the chart and time intervals along the bottom. Draw a line across the chart for each step, starting at the planned beginning date and ending at the completion date of that step.

GANTT CHARTS

Some parallel steps can be carried out at the same time with one taking longer than the other. This allows some flexibility for the start of the shorter step, as long as the plan has it finished in time to follow in subsequent steps. This situation can be shown with a dotted line continuing on to the line when the step must be completed.

When the Gantt chart is finished, you will be able to see the minimum total of time for the project, the proper sequence of steps and which steps can be underway at the same time.

You can add to the usefulness of a Gantt chart by also charting actual progress. This is usually done by drawing a line in a different colour below the original line to show the actual beginning and ending dates of each step. This allows you to quickly assess whether or not the project is on schedule.

Gantt charts are limited in their ability to show the interdependencies of activities. In projects where the steps flow in a simple sequence of events, they can portray adequate information for project management. However, when several steps are underway at the same time and a high level of interdependency exists among the various steps, PERT diagrams (discussed later) are a better choice.

PLANNING THE PROJECT

GANTT CHARTS

EXAMPLE

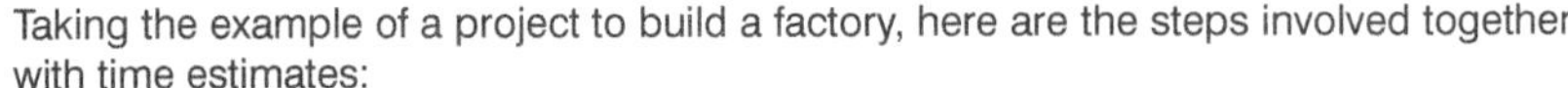
Taking the example of a project to build a factory, here are the steps involved together with time estimates:

Project steps	Days
1. Draw working plans	15
2. Obtain building permit	16
3. Form/pour foundation	5
4. Frame walls and roof	5
5. Install roofing	5
6. Install windows	1
7. Install exterior cladding	10
8. Paint exterior	3
9. Install electrical wiring	10
10. Install heating/air conditioning	5
11. Insulate	5
12. Install plasterboard	5
13. Install interior doors and trim	5
14. Paint interior	3
15. Install electrical fixtures	2
16. Clean up	3
17. Install floor covering	2
18. Hand over to client (ceremony)	1
Project duration	**85**
Project resource	**101**

GANTT CHARTS

EXAMPLE (Cont'd)

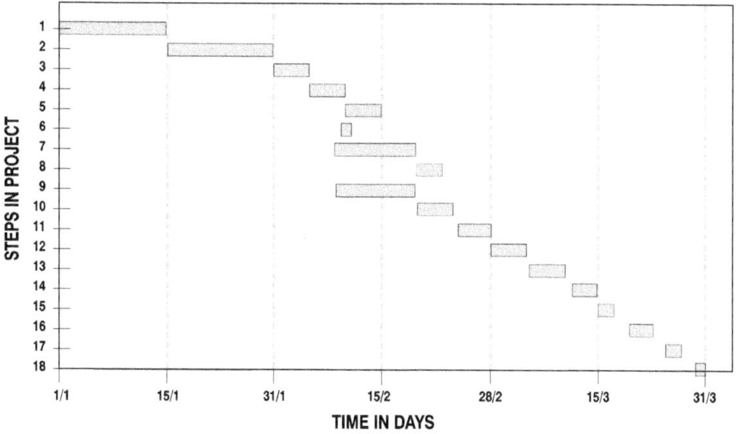

STEPS IN PROJECT

1
2
3
4
5
6
7
8
9
10
11
12
13
14
15
16
17
18

1/1 15/1 31/1 15/2 28/2 15/3 31/3

TIME IN DAYS

Note that activities 5, 6, 7 & 9 can occur in parallel so only the higher figure of 10 days gets added to the project's duration.

Therefore 16 days (5+1+10) comes off the total of resource days to identify the duration as 85 days.

PERT DIAGRAMS

PERT stands for **P**rogramme **E**valuation and **R**eview **T**echnique. Simple yet effective, PERT diagrams are used to plan out a project and have been used successfully for decades. They are a more sophisticated form of planning than Gantt charts, and appropriate for projects with many steps. They are known by several names, amongst them:

- Critical Path Analysis (CPA)
- Critical Path Method (CPM)
- Network Analysis (NA)
- Logic Diagrams

The key role of the PERT diagram is to indicate, in a very visual manner, the:

- Logical sequence of activities in a project
- Critical activities in a project
- Relationships between activities
- Time-scales involved
- Amount of spare time (known as float) in a project
- Opportunity to adjust resources to affect outcomes

PLANNING THE PROJECT

PERT DIAGRAMS

RECORDING THE PLAN

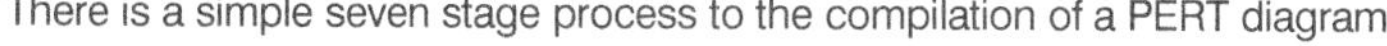
There is a simple seven stage process to the compilation of a PERT diagram:

1. Compile an Activity Schedule
2. Assess the relationship between activities
3. Compile the Nodes
4. Draw the links of the diagram
5. Enter the Finish Times
6. Assess the Critical Path
7. Calculate the time-scale and float

1. Compile an **Activity Schedule**

The Activity Schedule details the following aspects of the project:

- Activity
- Time-scale or duration
- Relationship with other activities

The next page illustrates what an Activity Schedule will look like.

PERT DIAGRAMS

STAGE 1: COMPILING AN ACTIVITY SCHEDULE

We will use an everyday example to illustrate how the schedule is compiled. If we regard making a cup of tea as a project, let's look at all the activities that could be involved and assess the time each might need. We will assume adding milk or sugar comes at a later stage.

ACTIVITY NUMBER	ACTIVITY	DURATION	RELATIONSHIP
01	Fill the kettle with water	30 seconds	
02	Heat kettle	180 seconds	
03	Take out pot for tea	20 seconds	
04	Take out tea	20 seconds	
05	Take out spoon	20 seconds	
06	Put tea in pot	20 seconds	
07	Take out cup	20 seconds	
08	Add hot water to pot	40 seconds	
09	Allow tea to brew	150 seconds	
10	Pour tea into cup	30 seconds	
11	Stir tea	10 seconds	

PLANNING THE PROJECT

PERT DIAGRAMS

STAGE 2: ASSESS THE RELATIONSHIPS BETWEEN ACTIVITIES

The next stage in completing the schedule is to assess the chronological relationships between each activity. Is there an activity that must have been completed before another one can start? Our completed Activity Schedule for making tea will now look like this:

ACTIVITY NUMBER	ACTIVITY	DURATION	RELATIONSHIP
01	Fill the kettle with water	30 seconds	
02	Heat kettle	180 seconds	Follows 01
03	Take out pot for tea	20 seconds	
04	Take out tea	20 seconds	
05	Take out spoon	20 seconds	
06	Put tea in pot	20 seconds	Follows 03, 04 & 05
07	Take out cup	20 seconds	
08	Add hot water to pot	40 seconds	Follows 02 & 06
09	Allow tea to brew	150 seconds	Follows 08
10	Pour tea into cup	30 seconds	Follows 07 & 09
11	Stir hot drink	10 seconds	Follows 05 & 10

PLANNING THE PROJECT

PERT DIAGRAMS

STAGE 3: COMPILE THE NODE

A Node is a simple, clear method for displaying all the essential information in the relevant place. Each activity will have one: it is merely a box with five component parts as here:

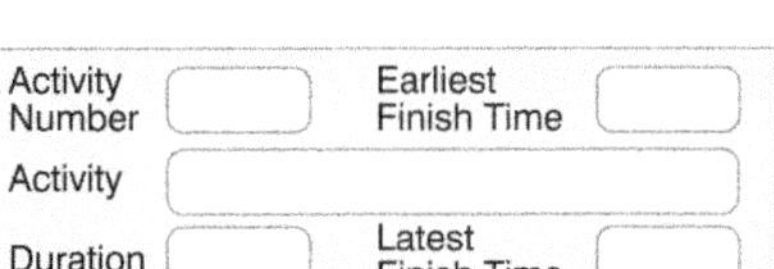

For reasons that will become evident, until we draw out the PERT diagram we cannot complete the finish time information. We can, however, complete the remaining information for each of the **Start Activities**, which from our schedule will be:

Fill the kettle with water
Take out pot for tea
Take out tea
Take out spoon
Take out cup

These are Start Activities because our Activity Schedule indicates that they are not dependent on any other activity having taken place before they can start. At this stage, we are not constrained by the logistics of resources merely by the relationship of one activity to any other.

PERT DIAGRAMS

STAGE 3: COMPILE THE NODE

As an example, the Node for *taking out the tea* will look like this:

04	
Take out tea	
20	

A helpful way to facilitate the next stage is to represent each Node on a post-it note, so that you can move it around the diagram and explore the process for effectiveness.

PERT DIAGRAMS

STAGE 4: DRAW THE LINKS OF THE DIAGRAM

All our Start Activities begin in a vertical stack on the left-hand side of our diagram (see page 78). This assumes that **they can happen in parallel**, though the extent of this will only be fully apparent once the top and bottom boxes on the right-hand side are completed. For the moment however, it helps to imagine a timeline running across the page from left to right.

The project plan will develop to the right of these Start Activity Nodes, beginning with the introduction of activity 02 to the right of activity 01, a relationship identified earlier from the schedule. Activity 06 (Put tea in pot) will appear below activity 02 and to the right of activities 03, 04 and 05. Draw lines to link the Nodes appropriately.

The next stage will be to complete the Nodes by entering the missing Finish Times in the respective boxes, once the connecting lines (or pathway) are drawn on the diagram.

PERT DIAGRAMS

STAGE 5: ENTER FINISH TIMES

The **Earliest Finish Time** (EFT) is the accumulated time working across the diagram from left to right. The EFT for activity 01 *filling the kettle* is 30 seconds. Activity 02 follows (see schedule) and takes 180 seconds. Therefore the earliest time that it can finish *within the overall process* is 30 + 180 = 210 seconds. As activity 08 follows 02, the EFT for 08 will be 30+180+ 40= 250 seconds. In this way, the duration of each activity is accumulated as time passes from left to right across the page. Where a set of concurrent activities links in (as with Start Activities), the highest of the EFTs in the set is carried forward to create the new EFT, by adding it to the duration of the new activity.

The **Latest Finish Time** (LFT) is calculated by working backwards (ie, from right to left) from the final activity (stirring the drink). At this point the EFT is 440 seconds: the LFT here will coincide with the EFT, as the **latest** time that activity 11 should finish is when all the activities have been completed in their allotted time. For activity 11 to finish on time, the LFT for activity 10 has to leave 10 seconds to stir the drink. The LFT in the Node for activity 10 will therefore be 430 seconds (440 – 10) and so it continues from right to left, subtracting the duration of each activity from its LFT.

PERT DIAGRAMS

STAGES 6 & 7

Stage 6 Assess the Critical Path

The Critical Path can be identified as the longest chain of activities reading from left to right. You can confirm the critical activities by comparing their EFT with the LFT in the Node; the Critical Path is the sequence of Nodes in which the EFT for each Node matches its LFT.

It is often denoted on diagrams using a symbol along the lines or a particular colour.

Stage 7 Calculate the time-scale and float

If we add up the duration of all the activities in our completed Activity Schedule, it might suggest the project of making a cup of tea will take 540 seconds. However, by compiling the Activity Schedule and drawing up the diagram, we can clearly see that the actual time needed is 440 seconds (7 minutes and 20 seconds), a saving of nearly two minutes.

Those activities not on the Critical Path will have a lower figure for the EFT than the LFT - this difference between the two figures is the float time. So, if it only takes 20 seconds to take out the tea (activity 04) but you don't actually need to have it ready until the 190th second, there are 170 seconds of float time available during which that activity can take place. Failure to complete it by the 190th second will affect the Critical Path.

PERT DIAGRAMS

THE APPLICATION

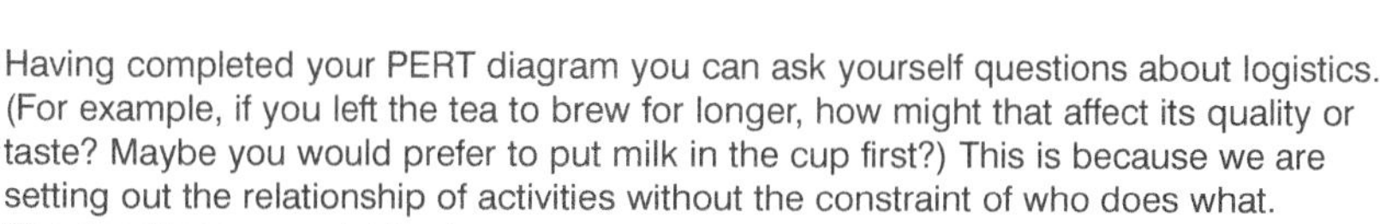

Having completed your PERT diagram you can ask yourself questions about logistics. (For example, if you left the tea to brew for longer, how might that affect its quality or taste? Maybe you would prefer to put milk in the cup first?) This is because we are setting out the relationship of activities without the constraint of who does what. The questions you might ask are:

- Can one person carry out all the activities or is more than one required?
- How can the float time be used productively?
- Is 440 seconds acceptable? Can we save time by using a higher kilowatt kettle?
- What if we want to put milk in before pouring the tea?

You are looking at a plan. Plans are for adapting to suit the circumstances, but the best plans start with best practice rather than with existing limitations!

Once you've answered your questions you can redraw the diagram if necessary, remembering to recalculate the EFT and LFT as you might affect the Critical Path. This diagram provides the basis then for developing Gantt charts and for reviewing against, as the actual project unfolds.

PERT DIAGRAMS

EXAMPLE

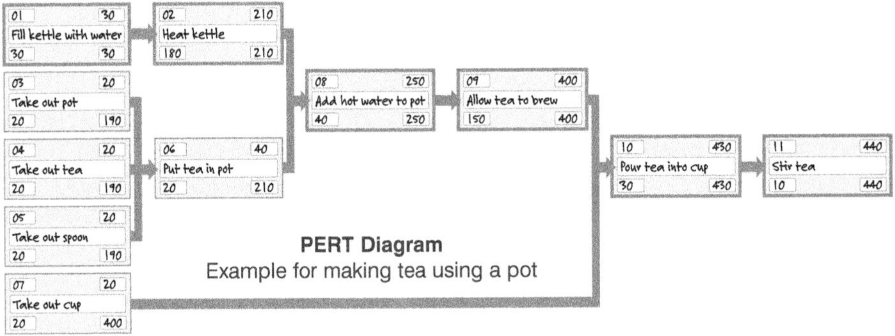

01 30
Fill kettle with water
30 30

02 210
Heat kettle
180 210

03 20
Take out pot
20 190

04 20
Take out tea
20 190

05 20
Take out spoon
20 190

06 40
Put tea in pot
20 210

07 20
Take out cup
20 400

08 250
Add hot water to pot
40 250

09 400
Allow tea to brew
150 400

10 430
Pour tea into cup
30 430

11 440
Stir tea
10 440

PERT Diagram
Example for making tea using a pot

Where activities can occur in parallel, the higher time accumulation is incorporated into the Critical Path.

The Critical Path (boxes outlined in bold) is where the Earliest Finish Time coincides with the Latest Finish Time (shown here in seconds).

PROJECT MANAGEMENT TOOLS

Take care, it is easy to get bogged down in the mechanics of planning a project.

There are excellent software tools such as Microsoft Project, Primavera SureTrak, Prince2 and Agile, which allow you to plan to any level of detail, but beware:

- A plan is a statement of intent not a destination in itself (as we move through different examples, see which tool suits your project best)
- A plan is important but it can be changed as the situation changes
- The software will not manage the project on its own but is there to help you manage it
- Plans and charts will not provide the leadership – that will come from you too

ALLOWING FOR MILESTONES

When scoping the project we talked about the importance of measurable outcomes. The plan must be geared towards achievement of all outcomes, with milestones identified en route to keep you on track. Don't leave the measurement until it's too late to adjust! Milestones can be identified on the PERT diagram as the points where activities are completed on the Critical Path.

"What gets measured gets done", Tom Peters

Some notable 'faux pas' include:

- **The development of a tolling system for cars wanting to enter Singapore city:** devised by a firm from another country, where motorists drive on the right-hand side, the toll booths are located in the wrong place. Consequently, drivers have to lean over the passenger side of the vehicle or get out to reach the booth!
- **A new rail network in the UK:** the new trains purchased were not of the right gauge for the track.

Don't take all you are told at face value – always check with a third party.

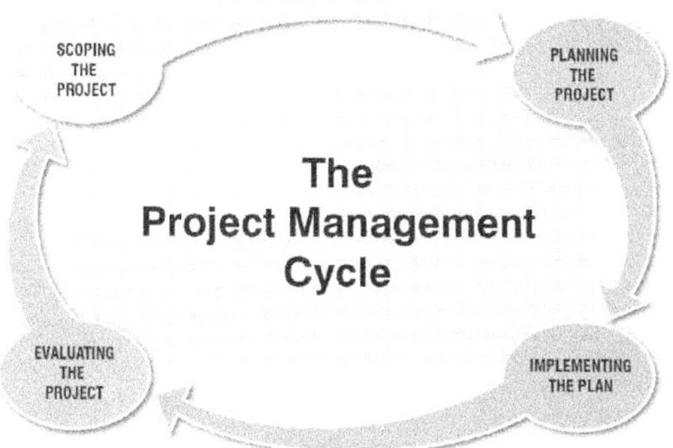

IMPLEMENTING THE PLAN

IMPLEMENTING THE PLAN

PROJECT MANAGEMENT CYCLE: STEP 3

Planning the work is one thing; working the plan is another. The trick is to keep as close to the original plan as possible, assuming, of course, that it was put together along the scoping guidelines we recommended earlier.

Implementing actions will involve:

- Applying the plan and working with team members and end-users
- Monitoring at check points (milestones) to make sure that the objective is being achieved
- Resolving problems as they occur (plans can change and may be permitted to go off track to a certain extent, as long as the objective is achieved by the end)

CONTROL POINT IDENTIFICATION CHARTS

Implementation should focus on the achievement of agreed outcomes, so that if a problem is encountered with the plan, other courses of action can be employed. Use the framework shown right to explore and record the need for contingencies, so that you are ready if they are needed.

Control element	What is likely to go wrong?	How and when will I know?	What will I do about it?
Quality			
Cost			
Time			
Quantity			

Hindsight can teach you that you underestimated the resources required, so always include contingency in your demands for money, manpower, etc.

TEAM CULTURES

Understanding the culture of the organisation, and that of the project team, can have a significant impact on the success of implementing plans.

Where would your organisation culture feature on this chart?

Organisation culture	Closed	Part open	Fully open
GOALS	are announced	are communicated	are agreed on
INFORMATION	is a status symbol	traded with like goods	exists in abundance
MOTIVATION	is manipulative	focused on the needs of the staff	has identification as its goal
DECISIONS	are only taken from above	partly delegated	fall on staff level
MISTAKES	are only made by staff	responsibility taken for	can be made
CONFLICTS	are unwelcome	are mastered	represent chances for innovation
CONTROL	comes from above	is partly delegated	self-control
MANAGERIAL STYLE	authoritarian, patriarchal	co-operative	ad hoc
AUTHORITY	wants obedience	wants co-operation	wants partnership
MANAGER	absolute ruler	problem-solver, decision-maker	strategist for change

PARTICIPATION

Seek participation in the formation of strategic goals – get opinion formers on your side!

- Conduct a one-hour training session on the subject of understanding change, so that attendees see the value of participation
- Soft issues are important to most businesses, and performance of people matters
- Change is about hearts and minds
- Look at issues as a process, not which department should do what!
- Hierarchies should be unimportant; there may be too much to do to allow a 'tell' culture to exist
- Rivalry is unimportant and disappears when the team work together to achieve the end goal

COLLECTIVE DECISION-MAKING

Project teams should take collective decisions and implement them by taking responsibility for their actions.

- Decisions need to be taken collectively so that you can be sure you are all saying the same thing no matter which forum (eg: training courses on management of change, team-building and technical cross-skilling courses) you are addressing
- This also applies to departmental team meetings, site presentations, corporate core team briefings, etc
- Encourage contributions of articles in all forms of corporate communications (eg: house magazines) so that the project is not seen as a faceless wonder
- Decision-makers must be accountable for the successful implementation of their decision
- When implementing, be the eyes and ears for the whole project team; remember to report back all the information gained - unfiltered and without any political 'flavouring' either
- Take feedback on a variety of project issues; relay it to the appropriate area and ensure that remedial action is taken where required
- Assume nothing

REDUCING HUMAN ERROR

PAUSE POINTS

On a project with a global bank to reduce human error in IT maintenance, it soon became apparent that many of the problems were embedded in the procedures engineers were following. They were so conditioned to following 'inputs' that they'd lost sight of the 'outcomes' which were to be achieved at key stages.

Atul Gawande's book, *The Checklist Manifesto,* recommends the use of Pause Points, which provide an opportunity at significant stages of an activity to determine that everything is exactly as it should be at that point. At the bank we used workshops to identify and define our Pause Points.

The application in hospitals particularly resonated with me because of two personal experiences. During major surgery in my teens I was conscious for several hours, hearing the dialogue in the operating theatre; on a separate occasion, during minor surgery, the incision for a lung drain was made before I had been given any anaesthetic.

Imagine how reassured I felt recently, when undergoing yet more major surgery, to know that operating theatres in the UK have these Pause Points, which they refer to as 'Time Out'.

REDUCING HUMAN ERROR

PAUSE POINTS

My conclusion, when working with clients to reduce human error, is that while we can never eradicate errors being made, we can prevent their consequences being passed down the process.

When the incision was made on me without anaesthetic, hierarchy had got in the way. I was in a military hospital where my surgeon was a Colonel - he walked into a side room where a Corporal and a Private had been setting up for the surgery. They saw him probing my chest with scalpel in hand but neither broke rank to prevent the incision and subsequent panic.

"What's happened?! Has he not had the anaesthetic?" asked the Colonel.
"No!" the lower ranks replied in unison. So the Colonel asked, *"Why not?"*
"You hadn't instructed us to give it", came the subordinate response.

This would have been so easy to fix. Gawande, himself a surgeon, proposes removing hierarchy in operating theatres so that an assistant can spot and correct errors made by senior surgeons (such as contaminating their gloves by wiping their own brow). Everyone is an equal when Pause Points are checked.

REDUCING HUMAN ERROR

PAUSE POINTS

We can identify Pause Points by noting previous errors or anticipated ones and restating them as a positive, desired outcome. In the example below, we see (continuing the hospital setting) what the Pause Points should look like at the Pre-incision stage; other stages are likely to be Pre-closure and Pre-departure.

Potential errors in the operating theatre:

- Patient not correctly anaesthetised
- Allergic reactions
- Wrong side of body operated on
- Correct equipment not available
- Infections from equipment
- Wrong blood supply

Therefore, the checklist at the pre-incision Pause Point will be:

- ✔ The patient has been successfully anaesthetised – evidence can confirm this
- ✔ Any patient peculiarities (allergies, etc) have been researched & communicated
- ✔ The incision point is correctly indicated and supported by triage notes
- ✔ Adequate, appropriate and sterile equipment is suitably laid out for the procedure
- ✔ Steps have been maintained to remove infections
- ✔ The correct blood group is identified and adequate blood supply is at hand

REDUCING HUMAN ERROR

CHECK OUTCOMES

Checklists are often used to monitor progress, and this was the case at the global bank where we were exploring issues with repetitive errors on IT maintenance. The mistake, however, was using the checklist to confirm that inputs had been carried out rather than that outcomes had been achieved. We covered outcomes earlier in 'Scoping the Project' and they provide the measure for any activity.

For example, checking that 'the patient has been given anaesthetic' (an input) is not the same as checking that "the patient has been successfully anaesthetised" (an outcome). There should always be evidence to examine to confirm an outcome!

IT Maintenance teams showed a lack of understanding of the consequential impact of any errors.... until we began expressing outcomes and identifying relevant evidence as the measure. Such an approach was estimated to have saved the bank over £90,000 in rework costs alone over the next 12 months: that saving was significantly enhanced when the impact on end-users was taken into account.

FIRE PREVENTION MEASURES

The best project managers are not the ones fighting the fires but the ones who take the trouble to prevent them starting in the first place.

So, if delivery of a key resource is critical to the ongoing timeframe, why wait to see if it arrives? Better to check with the provider's schedule a few days beforehand. What else on the 'critical path' can be chased up in advance?

Think, then, of your 5Ms (see earlier in this chapter) and 7Ss (see Evaluating the Project) whose ingredients may impact on your project. Might there be a potential fire-starter in there?

Similarly, watch out that your project doesn't start any fires elsewhere.

IMPLEMENTING THE PLAN

PROGRESS REPORTING

Keeping everyone informed of progress to date is a necessary activity of implementing. The purpose of reporting back is to highlight events significantly different from expectations rather than provide a diary account of all the period's happenings.

- For weekly/monthly progress reports use the **KISS** technique: **K**eep **I**t **S**hort and **S**imple
- Include bad news. Reports only need to state what has changed and what has been achieved. This is sometimes known as exception reporting
- One-to-one progress meetings are useful for project members to iron out micro issues (strategic issues should be left to the group meetings)
- Group project meetings should be held once a week face-to-face. An example for a meeting agenda is shown here

AGENDA
(5 mins per team member)

HR
Training
Premises
IT
Branches rolling out phase by phase
Operations and methods
Implementation team
Meeting critique (5 mins)

Rotating chair and secretary
Meeting max 50 mins

IMPLEMENTING THE PLAN

KEEP COMMUNICATION VISIBLE!

Many companies that have now restructured their customer contact centres use electronic displays to show how often and how quickly the phones are being answered, and to show performance against targets. Outstanding work by the back-office teams is also recorded: on whiteboards, intranets or even through social media in some cases.

It is important that all members of the team – especially those working remotely – as well as visiting clients and customers can see that service is taken seriously. Project teams really want the changes to be visible, practical, everyday enhancements to real-life work.

Everyone should be involved in discussing the best visible places as a project group. Each team should make its own choice, pointing out the pros and cons and overcoming objections such as 'big brother is watching you'. Any changes made by the implementation team should be introduced as an office benefit rather than as a threat.

Each member of the team should be responsible for implementing a part of the project whether on site or across functional boundaries. This will ensure that the project team is accountable!

FEEDBACK

HELPER is a simple process for providing feedback:

H ear each member's contribution
E laborate with additional positive examples
L ook at all members' ideas for improvement
P romote additional suggestions for improvement
E mpower the team: don't dictate
R ecognise overall positive behaviours, results and contributions

DESIGN & BUILD

Keeping control of the key outcomes of the project is only possible when the designer actually implements the plan. The 'design & build' technique works because the project team understand the constraints (site, organisation, available resources) and formulate their plan accordingly. Pragmatic, perhaps, but there are benefits as these examples demonstrate:

- It is said that Christopher Wren was present throughout the construction of St. Paul's Cathedral in London. He did not let the builders change his specification without recourse to him.
- In a major new London hospital, expensive porter trolleys that moved patients from the accident and emergency department to the operating theatre were too wide for the corridor doors. It was discovered later that no one had thought to check the specifications with the porters, even though the administration, medical and technical teams had all been consulted. If one trolley had been walked through, the problem could have been identified and resolved with little time and cost (see 'milestones' in the previous chapter). As it was, it became a toss up as to whether it was cheaper to change the trolleys or the doors!

PROVIDING TRAINING & SUPPORT

"In a changing world some things remain the same ... cock-ups."

Anon

It is essential that attention is given to the education and training of all who may be affected by the project, not just those who are directly working on it.

- Use attitude surveys to get a 'fix' on current attitudes and to identify where the focus of the education (and perhaps even of the project) may be needed
- Provide timetables, Gantt charts and other support material to keep everyone with you

THE CHANGE PROCESS

The implementation phase of some projects may take months, or even years.

An adaptation of Elizabeth Kubler-Ross's bereavement counselling model provides the language which the people in an organisation can use to identify where they are with the change. There are four stages:

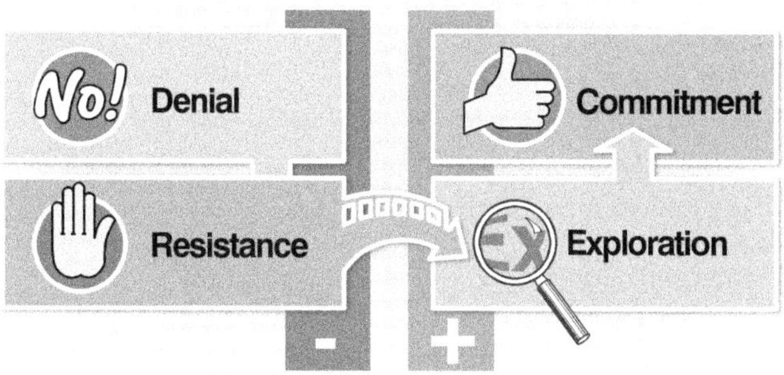

THE CHANGE PROCESS

DENIAL

- This can be explained as the ostrich phase or the bad dream: "I will wake up tomorrow and this will all have been a bad dream". Change is painful to all; it's just a matter of degree.
- It can be expressed in physical, emotional, logical and highly illogical ways to others: "The company will see the error of its ways. We will stop this working. It is impossible to run the department/branch without me. Other companies tried all these changes and found they did not work. Why do we always follow the failures of old, clapped-out theory?"

These outbursts, which will be familiar to many, are examples of what is said once the change is announced.

THE CHANGE PROCESS

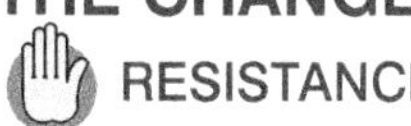

RESISTANCE

- This is the guerrilla warfare phase when we all feel like rebelling. We are outside our comfort zone and lash out at all people, things, views and ideas with which we feel uncomfortable.
- We hear things like: "Why me? Why must I change? No research has been done." All the anger that is felt by the individual or their peer group comes to the surface, if the organisation allows it to. In fact it is critically important to allow this to happen, though in a controlled way. Perhaps a revisit to the Stakeholder Analysis will help you anticipate and address some of the issues that are causing the resistance. As someone once said, "Let the bad out so that the good may come in".
- If the lid is held down the consequences will be more disastrous, as the staff that remain after the changes will be looking to sabotage the change. This applies to all levels of the company, up to the boardroom.

THE CHANGE PROCESS

SAYING GOODBYE TO THE PAST (BRIDGE TO STAGE 3)

- At some time there is a letting go, saying goodbye to the past. While not forgetting, people may forgive or, at least, understand the reasons why the changes had to be made.
- In bereavement terms, this could be seen as a wake. One organisation encouraged and paid for a good party before a new amalgamated branch was opened, so there was a clear break in time. It allowed the staff to, quite literally, 'let their hair down'. The staff and management were told that this was a part of the change process and that this was why it was being held. Openness again is a crucial part of the new organisation.
- Communicating with all people all of the time cannot be underestimated. As with justice, it must not only be done, but it must be seen to be done.
- Evidence of showing a degree of humanity during the process destroys the platform for the negative opinion formers.

THE CHANGE PROCESS

EXPLORATION

- Once people feel that the worst is over there is a period of adjustment. This is when the questions emerge. These could be asked in a variety of contexts and venues. Informally, questions may arise by the coffee machine, in the restaurant, canteen or lift, during shared bus or car journeys, on the e-mail or telephone or, most commonly, at the work desk. Since informal contact is as important as the formal team briefing or line management communication, it too needs to be managed.
- We will believe or disbelieve what we hear, depending upon the regard we have for the communicator.
- Time must be given to answering the questions, however ridiculous, as little if any work will be done until the information is given. 'Walking the talk' is essential.

THE CHANGE PROCESS

COMMITMENT/ACCEPTANCE

- There is now an acknowledgement that things have changed and the new system is here to stay
- It does not necessarily mean unbridled enthusiasm
- The days of resisting and wanting to sabotage the change are over
- Commitment is the aim and goes beyond Acceptance (which Kubler-Ross saw as the final stage). We will see people actively working with the change as opposed to not fighting it

GROUP NORMS

As well as four stages of the change process, Tuckman's theory has it that the group, work-based or otherwise, will follow the four stages of development shown below.

Forming The group first gets together with its common aim.

Storming A short while after the group forms, aims and objectives are questioned and the group experiences conflict from within, perhaps because some activities are being duplicated, or even ignored, and communications break down.

Norming Because of the conflict, policy and procedures are drawn up and agreed by the consensus of the group so that expectations are clarified and managed.

Performing The group adheres to the policy and procedures and works effectively towards its aim.

You can expect your own project team to pass through these stages though, with foresight, you can be prepared and control what is controllable!

GROUP NORMS

THE CHANGE MODEL

Simply by overlaying the stages of group development onto the change process grid, we can see that when we undergo change it has the same effect as making us start again. Effective project management should, therefore, involve facilitating the transition of those affected by the change.

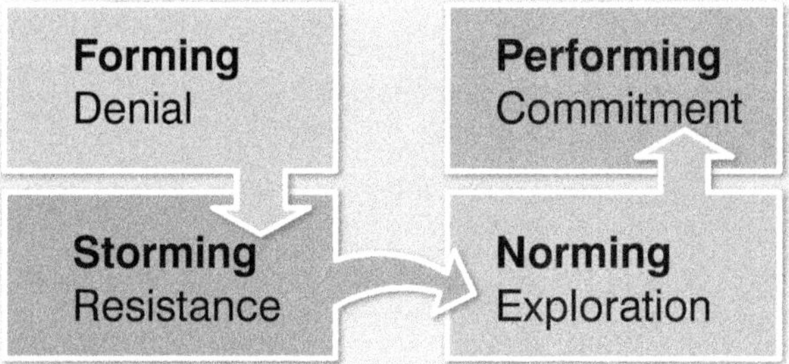

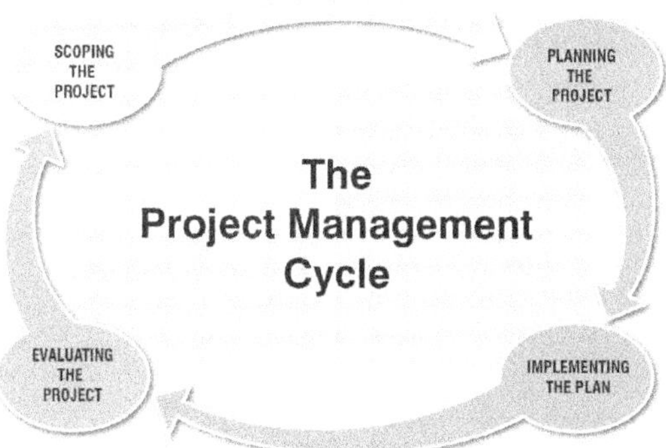

EVALUATING THE PROJECT

EVALUATING THE PROJECT

PROJECT MANAGEMENT CYCLE: STEP 4

The act of reviewing the plan really begins during the implementation phase, but at the end of the project we also want to look at the lessons to be learned from how it was carried out, and to see whether its completion has had the desired effect.

There are several ways to review a project:

1. McKinsey's 7S model of change
2. Questioning (What went well? What did not go well? What should we change?)
3. Traffic light technique

EVALUATING THE PROJECT

MCKINSEY'S 7S MODEL

Consider the impact of change upon these 7Ss (we are looking at this after the project, but the same model could be used at the planning stage):

Strategy	The vision and business plan – is there a new direction and a need to replan?
Systems	Computer and manual processes – are we more efficient; where can we improve?
Staff	The affected parties – are they familiar with the changes and have they accepted them?
Skills	Future knowledge and skills needed – what are the training or recruitment implications?
Style	Methods of communication – are there fewer misunderstandings; has technology gone too far?
Shared values	Culture and ethos – are we contradicting or losing sight of who we are?
Structure	Reporting lines and framework – is decision-making enhanced and duplication of effort avoided?

Are there other issues to be addressed now?

QUESTIONING/TRAFFIC LIGHT TECHNIQUE

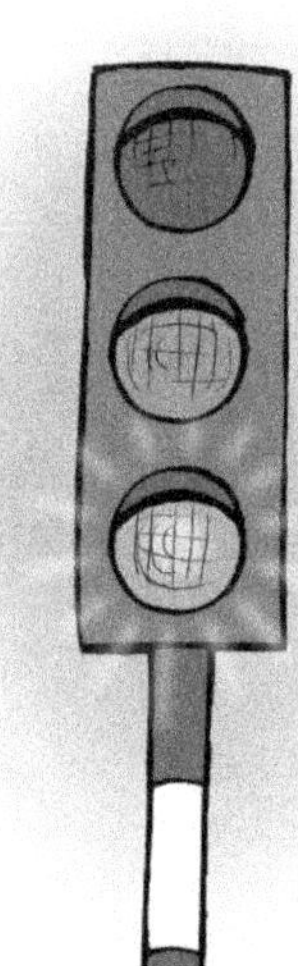

Ask yourself, the team and the project sponsor:

- What went well in the project?
- What did not go well in the project?
- What would we change for the next project?
- What was missing, or missed but not foreseen?

Alternatively, apply the traffic light technique:

Red - What should we stop doing?

Amber - What do we need to consider adapting for future use?

Green - What did we do well that should be continued next time?

EVALUATING THE PROJECT

PROJECT MANAGEMENT TOOLS

The very tools that formed the basis of the project plans now become the basis for review. Typically, these would be:

- Gantt
- SWOT
- PESTLE
- PERT
- Pause Points
- Control point identification charts
- 5M Analysis

All have been discussed in earlier chapters. How accurate did they prove to be and where could changes be made for the future?

EVALUATING THE PROJECT

PRINCE2

Let's see how the 4 Elements of Prince2 – Principles, Themes, Processes and Tailoring – devolve and link to the tools shown in this book:

7 PRINCIPLES

Business reason – we explore PESTLE and the force-field drivers

Learn from experience – have regular reviews and don't hide mistakes

Defined roles & responsibilities – outcomes determined and allocated

Managed stages – milestones, pause points, critical path

Exception – performance measures, pause points

Focus on products – clear descriptions of what good looks like, stakeholder analysis

Tailored to the project environment – force-field, Gantt charts, PERT

PRINCE2

7 THEMES

Business case – stakeholder analysis, force-field analysis with WIIFM?

Organisation – scoping document (time, cost, quality, quantity), 5Ms and 7Ss, Belbin,

Quality – outcomes and use of pause points to reduce human error

Plans – inputs linked to outcomes, resources (5Ms), timeframes

Risk – stakeholder analysis & mapping, pause points, fire prevention list

Change – Kubler-Ross and overcoming resistance

Progress – progress reports and group project meetings; use of wall-boards

PRINCE2

7 PROCESSES

Starting up – apply scoping tools, clarify outcomes, identify skill-sets

Directing – participation, Johari window, 7 deadly sins

Initiating – leader v manager, ENTHUSIASM, team framework

Managing a stage boundary – fire prevention list, pause points

Controlling a stage – control point identification and pause points

Managing product delivery – check performance against desired outcomes

Closing a project – scoping document, traffic lights, 7Ss, stakeholder analysis

TAILORING

This should be done in parallel to the 7 Principles, 7 Themes and 7 Processes, and captured in the outcomes being set. It could be too late to tailor everything in series; imagine designing and building an aircraft, taking it out of the hangar onto the runway and only then thinking about how you could train someone to fly it or maintain it. Flight simulators and service plans would need to be developed in parallel.

PROJECTING WITH PEOPLE

PROJECT LEADER OR PROJECT MANAGER?

The differences between leaders and managers are regularly debated in management development programmes. The debate applies equally to whether a project **requires** a manager or a leader.

The simple answer is that it requires both. The skill is in knowing which to do when. You also need to identify your particular aptitude. If the person accountable for delivering a successful project spends all their time in an office drawing up plans, then they may be good at managing but they won't be a good leader. By contrast, a person who primarily focuses on meeting and conversing with people may be a good leader, but one who fails to make use of the tools that help to manage.

The perspective that most people miss with the word *leader* is that it means there are followers. So ask yourself, 'what would get the team to follow?'

Do you have what it takes to choose when to lead and when to manage? The next page identifies some of the accepted views that differentiate the manager from the leader.

PROJECT LEADER OR PROJECT MANAGER?

Manager	Leader
Tells	Sells
Has a process	Has a vision
Administers	Innovates
Maintains within constraints	Develops to break free of constraints
Focuses on systems	Focuses on people
Relies on control	Inspires and motivates
Short-range view	Long-range view
Asks 'how and when?'	Asks 'what and why?'
Eye on the bottom-line	Eye on the horizon
Imitates	Creates
Accepts the status quo	Challenges the status quo
Does things right	Does the right things

JOHARI WINDOW

MODEL FOR SHARING INFORMATION

In order to capture the information in boxes B, C and D of the Johari window (next page) you need to improve your communication in any way you can. The better and more varied your communications are the smaller your 'unexplored' box will become, but you will never lose it completely. Here are some suggestions:

1. **Project review meetings** where you may wish to allocate team roles to look for the items or areas that they have Noticed, Felt, Want to Keep or Want to Change.
2. **One-to-ones** with each project member.
3. **Intranet** of all the team members' key thoughts, such as the use of a blog.
4. **Corridor meetings**.
5. **Telephone call catch ups**.
6. **Exception reporting**: 10 minute stand up meetings or via TV or voice conference where all comment on issues.

"You will never communicate perfectly but you may well be able to communicate less badly!"

JOHARI WINDOW

MODEL FOR SHARING INFORMATION

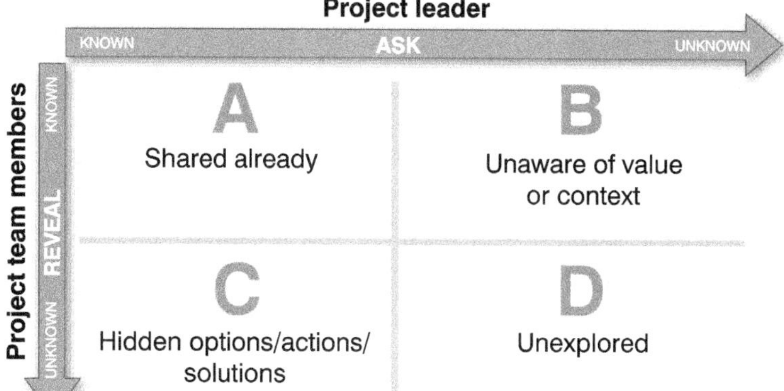

DAY ONE AS PROJECT LEADER

- Let everyone on the project know that no one is bigger than the project, and that each team member must be prepared to coach and be coached in new skills and take on the good as well as the bad parts of any task to complete the project
- Ensure everyone has access to the same technology and information hub, whether it's via an intranet, social media or whiteboards
- All team members need to meet each other at the start and identify the outcomes they will all share in. Roles and responsibilities need to be agreed. People need to feel proud that they have been included
- Dedicated team members must be paired with someone to ensure there is always cover in case of emergency or illness: the show must go on regardless!
- Share information – you never know what you may have that could be useful or valuable to another. Sharing information is the key to moving as swiftly and skilfully as possible and to keeping remote workers engaged with the wider team

THE 7 DEADLY SINS OF PROJECTS

1. **Scope creep** Recognise that every piece of work you get is a potential project and that people not directly affected by the project will want you to add things to it. Check with the sponsor before proceeding!
2. **Poor organisation of resources** Where team members work in disparate locations, communication problems can arise. There is no substitute for face-to-face meetings as they avoid misunderstandings; this is especially crucial at the start of a project.
3. **Poorly defined roles** Ensure the team knows who does what and who is responsible for what.
4. **Over-dependency** Members of the team must be able to double up for each other to ensure the project is not dependent on one person.
5. **Lack of agreed objectives** with the project sponsor – if there are any material changes ensure that these are agreed and the specification is altered. You can always change a plan but ensure that there is one!
6. **Poor documentation** Ensure that any desired outcomes or parts of a plan are written down so that there can be no argument.
7. **Overspending** Budget with estimates rather than 'guesstimates' and know who holds the purse strings, as there will always be a trade off between time and cost.

ADVICE TO A NEW PROJECT LEADER

- ✔ Keep all informed
- ✔ Agree time-scales and double them!
- ✔ Allow for contingencies in the planning stage (eg: holidays and delays in the decision-making process of the project's decider/sponsor)
- ✔ Use IT tools (eg: Microsoft Project, Primavera SureTrak, Prince2, Agile)
- ✔ Ensure your objectives are clear and check outcomes required!
- ✔ Be tenacious and trust the skills of the team
- ✔ Sell to and influence anyone who will help you (politics)
- ✔ Practise using tools (eg: Gantt and PERT) on everyday jobs at home and at work
- ✔ Get 'enough' research done – probably 80% will be enough
- ✔ Always consider the 'neighbours' – just as you would if any building work affected them – since change can usually instigate political piracy

SELL THE BENEFITS (WIIFM)

"It is easier for the losers to see what they will lose than the gainers to see how they will gain"

Machiavelli

- ✔ Concentrate on selling the project to people, particularly those it will affect
- ✔ Sell the benefits in terms of what it will do for them:
  - Will it save them time, effort, money, embarrassment and injury?
  - Will it enhance their skills?
- ✔ Arrange your audience into target groups so you can focus on the benefits they alone receive, whilst addressing their particular concerns

COMMUNICATE WITH ENTHUSIASM

Remember to **ENTHUS**.......................with plenty of **IASM**

- **E** — **Enthusiasm** As Emerson put it …'Nothing can be achieved without enthusiasm'.
- **N** — **Name** Not numbers – one leader described his day as….'a series of 5 minutes with each member of my team'…he had 100! Remember first names, not just e-mail addresses.
- **T** — **Trust** Unless project team members trust you they will not follow you. Trust comes from describing what you saw, not how you felt; identify the evidence to support what you say
- **H** — **Honesty** Remember the need to be fair, honest and confidential, either as an implementer or as a survivor.
- **U** — **Understanding** Check your understanding as well as theirs and build self-esteem.
- **S** — **Success** In a successful project team everyone contributes, everyone listens, everyone is courteous, everyone tells the truth, and everyone is supportive.

And above all remember that 'my' project will only succeed if

- **I** — I
- **A** — **Am**
- **S** — **Sold**
- **M** — **Myself**

OBSERVATIONS FROM EXPERIENCED PROJECT MANAGERS

- Project management normally means radical change for all involved including those making the changes
- The process affects each person in a different way
- Paternalism may give way to self-interest
- There is no magic formula to change management
- Perception is more important than reality
- Functional thinking is slow and departments or branches will only communicate from the top down or to a fellow worker if they are of the same grade
- Ideas get balked at constantly and 'steady as she goes' become the watch words
- Everyone knows that something must be done but not me and not now!
- New technology is often unused or ignored because its benefits have not been explained to the end-user, or training has been inadequate

MORALE : THE RIPPLE EFFECT

There are six ways to build **MORALE** and motivate your team through major change:

Myself — The best encouragement that you can give is your absolute undivided attention, your interest, your concentration, your time.

Openness — Communicate – a greeting, congratulations, a recommendation to someone else, a thank-you, etc.

Remember — People expect attention from you on returning from a trip to see a client/customer, on achieving a milestone, on doing overtime, etc.

Attention — A small surprise will do: flowers, a card, a smile, 'thanks', the ubiquitous cream buns, a personal letter, a box of sweets/biscuits on return from holiday – all unexpected attention.

Listen — Never refuse attention when someone asks for it. Children expect it but as adults we have been taught rejection. So, if we ask for attention (yes, some of us will have needed courage even to ask) we really need it! Never refuse!

Esteem — If you flatter without honesty, neither you nor the receiver will feel good about it. Your body language, and that of your team member, will clearly show what a fake you are!

ACTION PLANS

Show an interest in the people working with you on a project and they, in turn, will invest their interest in their work.

Use action plans, like the one shown here, to 'buy in' project members and for review purposes.

Three Month Action Plan

Name:

Team:

Direct Report:

I have set myself the following goals to achieve (these should be a mixture of business and personal):

Number	Goal (What?)	Action (What will I do?)	Time Scale (By when?)
1			
2			
3			
4			
5			
6			
7			
8			
9			
10			

PROJECT 'HIGHS' & 'LOWS'

Below are the responses of 20 project managers who were asked for their 'highs' and 'lows' when working on a project:

HIGHS

- Success at end
- Recognition
- Planning
- Discovering hidden talents
- Overcoming politics
- Clarifying objectives
- Taking calculated risks

- Letting go ... (after)
- Moving goal posts
- Outside environment changing
- Let down by team
- Computer corruption
- Delays outside our control

LOWS

FURTHER READING

Excellent books recommended by the authors:

- **Project Management** by Marion Haynes, Kogan Page
- **Take The Lead** by Boddy & Buchanan, Prentice Hall
- **Practical Project Management** by Dr. Richard Gould, Fenman
- **The Empowerment Pocketbook** by Mike Applegarth and Keith Posner, Management Pocketbooks
- **Management Teams – Why They Succeed or Fail** by Professor M. Belbin, Heineman
- **The Checklist Manifesto** by Atul Gawande, Profile Books
- **Prince 2 For Beginners** by Bryan Mathis, Createspace Independent Publishing Platform

About the Authors

Mike Applegarth Chartered FCIPD, has managed learning & development projects for a range of clients within sectors such as Total Facilities Management, Petrochemicals, Financial, Insurance, IT and Pharmaceutical, in addition to developing & piloting National Standards.

As well as leadership, sales and negotiation training, Mike trains in project management and has helped organisations identify their own processes, documentation and outcome measures, and reduce human error. In particular, participants learn just how much the day job benefits from scoping, planning, implementing and evaluating.

He is the author of 'How To Take A Training Audit' (a lead work in Pfeiffer's Practical Trainer Series) and, with Keith Posner, he has written two other pocketbooks. 'Leading Empowerment: A Practical Guide to Change' is his latest work, published by Elsevier.

Mike can be contacted at: Applegarth Training, Manfield House, Collins Gardens, Ash, Surrey GU12 6EP
Tel:+44 (0)1252 338517

Email: mike@applegarthtraining.co.uk

www.applegarthtraining.co.uk

Keith Posner LLB Hons, FCIPD ACIM FInstLM. Keith began his professional training career over 30 years ago at Nationwide Building Society. He then joined Allianz Cornhill Insurance and managed the specialist training function on their business process re-engineering project team.

Keith and his wife Sian formed Positive Perspective in 1995. Their team of consultants specialise in one-to-one executive coaching, and designing and delivering a wide range of individually tailored training programmes, including: Business Planning and Project Management, Stress Management, Life Balance, Leadership & Motivation, Selling & Negotiation Skills, Management of Change, Team Building, Career Development Centres and Communication & Empowerment.

Positive Perspective's client base includes managing directors, partners and senior managers from prominent global and national companies, notably within the utilities, financial and service sectors. With Mike Applegarth he has written two other pocketbooks, on empowerment and call centre customer care.

Keith can be contacted at: Positive Perspective,
The Coach House, Henfold Lane, South Holmwood, Dorking, Surrey RH5 4NX Tel: +44 (0)1306 88 89 90
Email: keith@positiveperspective.co.uk

www.positiveperspective.co.uk